MaeMae's
Grandmother
Book

Life Lessons for Our Grandchildren
(big people too)

Marilyn Tinnin (signature)

By Marilyn Tinnin

Foreword by Robert St. John

Printed in the United States of America

Cover photo © 2019 Deryll Stegall

Chapter sketches © Stacy Underwood

ISBN 978-1-64467-197-9

LifeStory Publishing
109 North State Street
Jackson, Mississippi 39202
601-594-0018

Spirituality. Devotional. Instructional. Family. Children.

Acknowledgements

Books don't write themselves. Even a well-intentioned writer with a passion for her message could never have managed to put pen to paper without the encouragement and expertise of an experienced editor. My deep gratitude to Joe Maxwell for believing I had something worthwhile to say and guiding me through the process. To Robert St. John, whose writing wit is every bit as sharp as his culinary skill, thank you for the perfect foreword. Stacy Greer Underwood's illustrations were like the icing on the cake! Her quick grasp of the message and her skill with pen and ink sketches gives new meaning to the old adage, "A picture is worth a thousand words." Thank you, too, to those who graciously read the unfinished manuscript and offered words of support—Shawn Edwards, Peggy Brown, Rose Flenorl, Terri Herring, Marsha Blackburn, Deborah Bryant, and Maggie Wade. Thank you to those who agreed to let me use their stories in telling mine: Gail Pittman, Susan Richardson, Grace Bateman Greene, Ginny Futvoye, Danny Fitzhugh, Robert Khayat, and Robert St. John. I am also grateful to my dear friend Bob Litro, who has stayed on me for years to get this done. He is a big believer in telling our stories and passing on our values. Thank you, Bob, for the frequent phone calls to hold me accountable!

Dedication

I lovingly dedicate this book to you, my thirteen amazing grandchildren. I am blessed to have two sets of amazing grands to love.

I never realized in my younger years how much I would love you or how much I would yearn to help you avoid any regret or mistake that might bring you sadness. Hopefully, a few of my life lessons might save you all some grief, but just in case you make a few choices that you wish you could reverse, I hope this little epistle helps you there, as well. Our God is such a better parent—or grandparent—than I could ever be because He knows how to take both our proud moments as well as our less than proud moments and turn them all into gold. He is a most redemptive God.

I am certainly not a theologian although I have tried, seeking counsel to be sure that there is no false advice in this book. I do know where my heart is, and it is all over each of you.

For Allie, Charlotte, Sutton, Marilyn Wilton, Vivi, and Smith—you each surprise me year after year with your talents, your creativity, and your very tender hearts. I love you to the moon and back, and I pray daily that you will grow to be as "wise as serpents and as gentle as doves" (Matthew 10:16). You will need wisdom to get through this world safely, and gentleness is a special strength that will keep your heart receptive to God and to others.

What joy, laughter… I mean hilarious laughter … you have all brought to me! What a totally unexpected delight it has been in my later years to see how each of you mirror different parts of your mom and dad, my babies that I nurtured from birth. I love watching their special traits show up in each of you.

For Katie, Bennett, Chase, Evan, Henry, Kenneth, and Allison—you have added such blessings to my life. I have called your mothers my "bonus babies" for a reason. They welcomed me into their hearts and homes when I married their dad, and they have blessed every day of my life since then. You are the blessing on top of that blessing, and you have made my life rich beyond my wildest dreams. I love you all. You are in my prayers and in my heart always.

Now to him who is able to keep you from stumbling and to present you blameless before the presence of his glory with great joy, to the only God, our Savior, through Jesus Christ our Lord, be glory, majesty, dominion, and authority, before all time and now and forever. Amen.

—*Jude: 1: 24, 25*

Foreword

By Robert St. John

My paternal grandmother, Eunice Holleman St. John, was the greatest influence in, and on, my life.

I have been a business owner for over 32 years and have worked in my chosen profession—the restaurant business—for almost 40 years. Over the decades, I have attended a dozens of business seminars and corporate conventions, where I have heard hundreds of speakers and experts shell out advice on what constitutes a successful life and career. All of those words, from all of those specialists in their fields, with all of their degrees, and all of the various letters, designations, and titles after their names pale in comparison to the lessons I learned from my grandmother in the first quarter century of my life.

Mam-Maw, as I called her, was an extremely intelligent, sweet, well-travelled, kind, compassionate, and caring Christian woman, who graduated as Valedictorian of her college, and spent a few years as a teacher before meeting my grandfather and becoming a full-time mother, dedicated church member, and civic-minded citizen.

She was probably one of the most selfless, pure, and good-hearted people I have known—a perfect example of a gracious southern lady. If the doors of Main Street United Methodist Church were open, she was there, and active. Within an hour after the last note of the doxology was hit on the massive pipe organ of the Sunday service, she somehow had a full spread on her formal dining room table ready for family and friends to enjoy. It seemed so effortless to her, probably because it was done out of unadulterated, selfless love and devotion to her family and friends. Those Sunday meals I enjoyed as a child are still the gold standard for me, and probably had a lot to do with the profession I chose—the hospitality industry.

In addition to being a gracious hostess and a model citizen, she was wise. And the wisdom came—not only from her innate instincts and intelligence, but—from living a devout Christian life, completely dedicated to Christ-centered principles and biblical teachings.

In my later college years, and during the early years after opening my first restaurant, I lived in a detached garage apartment behind her house. The apartment had been built for an uncle who never moved back to town. It served as a storage warehouse until I fixed it up and set up camp for seven years beginning in 1984. I lived in that one-room garage apartment until I was 30-years old. I loved it, and wouldn't have lived anywhere else, mainly because it was near my grandmother. She and I were able to spend a lot of time together— quality time—where she always gave me her complete and undivided attention.

Late at night, after the end of a long day working at the restaurant, I would drive down the alley to the garage behind her house. I could see her sitting in her chair in, what she called, "the sunroom," watching television or reading the paper. Many nights I would go inside the house and visit with her. We would spend 20-30 minutes talking about what each other had done during our day, or of family history. Then I would kiss her goodnight, excuse myself, and go out to the garage apartment. She loved those chats. I loved those chats. And I suspect she stayed up later than she wanted each night hoping I would come into the house for a visit.

Many nights I was tired after a rough day of kitchen work and didn't feel like a lengthy visit. Those nights I would go straight up to my garage apartment. Sometimes, feeling slightly guilty, I would peek through the blinds of my apartment across the driveway to the sunroom of her house to see if she was still sitting in her chair, waiting on me. She always was. Always. She would usually give it 15 minutes or so after she saw my car pull up to see if I was going to come inside for a visit, and then when I hadn't, she would turn off the light and go to bed.

As I sit here and write this today—almost three decades later—I can easily say that not going back inside of that house every single night to spend time with my grandmother every chance I had is my main life regret. Period. End of story. Nothing else even comes close in the regret category. It's not the girl that got away, or the business deal that never happened, or the money I lost on an investment. No. My number-one greatest regret is not spending more time with my grandmother when I had the chance. There is nothing more permanent than lost time with departed loved ones. I would give anything I own for one more 30-minute visit.

Marilyn Tinnin's grandchildren will never have that unending, aching regret. They have the book you hold in your hands. Her grandchildren, your grandchildren, and my future grandchildren will benefit from the principled wisdom and sage Christian advice contained within. All of the best societies through the ages are the ones that have passed faith, knowledge, and experience on to the next generation. Those life lessons are here in black and white, and we are all better for it.

Read on.

Table of Contents

The greatest legacy one can pass on to one's children and grandchildren is not money or other material things accumulated in one's life, but rather a legacy of character and faith.

— Billy Graham

Stop dreaming about your Bucket List and start living it.

— Annette White

Introduction

You are holding in your hand the first completed task on my Bucket List.

I retired earlier this year after a 17-year career as a most unlikely publisher and editor of a monthly Christian lifestyle magazine. I say unlikely because I lacked any legitimate credentials in journalism or business when I launched my midlife career. What I lacked in experience, I managed to make up in passion and a dogged determined work ethic. Not for one minute do I believe I would have enjoyed the success I did apart from God's grace and mercy. He answered many a prayer, bringing me associates whose gifts compensated for my deficits, complemented my vision, and provided friendship and advice day in and day out.

I absolutely loved my job. Writing the faith stories of others gave me a window into God's creative and myriad methods of pursuing His people. From successful governors, congressmen, and athletes to hardworking men and women in a regular everyday circle, I discovered again and again that our God is ever present. The great takeaway was that those who live with the greatest sense of peace and purpose are those who recognize that God's sovereignty knows no boundaries, and His love has no limits. Even when the road is rocky, His presence comforts and lights the path before us. He is not a neat little god that fits efficiently into the Sunday compartment of one's schedule. He invades all the parts of all our days. The God who gives breath so often pursues until He captures the whole heart.

Every person's story had its own vignettes—setting, scenes, circumstances and cast of characters. But in so many ways all those stories I got to tell were similar. Life can be brutal, but God is good. The Bible says, "As iron sharpens iron, so one person sharpens another" (Proverbs 27: 17).

I know that is true. Those who shared their very personal stories with me took me to a deeper place in my own relationship with the Lord. As the years sailed by, God took me through a few trials of my own. I found encouragement by recalling those personal stories of others. Although knowing God did not erase all the hard things or cure all the hurt, the certainty of His presence gave me strength and hope to just keep putting one foot in front of the other every day. I knew I was not alone.

When I eventually found myself on the other side of a trial, something in my heart was different. My relationship with my Heavenly Father was a bit more real and a lot more solid. Time after time, year after year, God has led me, counseled me, blessed me, comforted me, and proved to me that He is my refuge, fortress, and the Rock of Ages.

We live in strange times. The Postmodern era is an age dominated by secularism. The prevailing culture wants to remove any mention of God from the public square. For more than half my life it was common practice to open community events with prayer, to celebrate Christmas in public places with a nativity scene, or to light government buildings with crosses during Lent. None of those customs are commonplace anymore. It makes me sad.

Our world no longer seems to value the things I value— those things, I would add, are the things my parents and grandparents valued and tried to pass on to my generation. Today's mainstream thought does not take its wisdom from scripture; it does not run after God; and it does not promote the existence of absolute truth.

It alarms me that my grandchildren are growing up in a world where they hear one set of principles at home and a completely opposite set almost everywhere else. This grandmother prays two things for her grandchildren every single day. I pray that God would guard their hearts because scripture (Proverbs 4:23) says, "Above all else, guard your heart, for everything you do flows from it." And then I pray that God would grant them discernment so that they would recognize God's truth as well as Satan's deceptions.

Jesus's beloved disciple John wrote to one of his protégés in

3 John: "I have no greater joy than to hear that my children are walking in truth." That verse resonates in my heart and in the hearts of my close grandmother friends.

I am soberly aware of passing time and more conscious than ever that I do have an expiration date! My thirteen grandchildren range in age from three to fourteen. It is a safe bet that I will never have the opportunity to tell them one-on-one half the things I have written about here.

But I care—oh how I do care—about their values, their character, and their hearts! It is my hope that as life unfolds for each one of them, there might be an occasion here and there when they wonder, "Did MaeMae have anything to say about this?"

Maybe they will find the answer to that question within these pages.

And we know that all things work together for good to those who love God, to those who are called according to His purpose.

— Romans 8:28

Be faithful in small things because it is in them that your strength lies.

— Mother Teresa

Chapter 1

Remember to Pay Attention

Every day brings opportunities to experience God at work in your heart and in your life. Never forget that. Pay attention in the mundane moments and disappointing circumstances as well as in the moments when all is well because God is present in both.

A renowned theologian was teaching at prayer meeting years ago when I was a member at Christ United Methodist Church in Jackson. He had a wonderful way of making a point so simple you thought, "Why didn't I think of that already?" I have never forgotten what he said. "God never wastes anything in your life."

I could think of about ten things without even trying that I would have liked to erase from my past—choices I regretted because they were wrong as well as events that were so profoundly painful I still grieved them. Had God used those things in my life?

Psalm 139:16 says, "All the days ordained for me were written in your book before one of them came to be." God knew on the day of my birth everything there would ever be to know about me. He knew long before I learned how to break a rule and lie about it that I was going to do so. When I think about his "book" recording all my days, I wished I could either rewrite or omit a few chapters. The truth that overwhelms me, however, is that God the Father knew in the very beginning of my life what every single day would hold. Nothing catches God by surprise.

Our vision may be clouded at times, but God's never is. You know, I have lived through enough crises to believe that truth wholeheartedly. God always has *the right* plan in mind. I find that thought comforting.

If you can believe that He has a master plan for each of us, you might want to pay attention to every side road and detour in your journey. Every road connects to the next road. Every path leads to the one after it. Nothing is random.

When I look back over almost seven decades of life, I see clearly that the road from birth to this point had few straight lines. I imagine if my journey was a map, there would even be a few roads that seemed to go in circles. I see now that every point along the way had purpose although I did not always see that purpose at the time.

A prime example of God's design in the middle of something that did not even register as significant in the moment is the evolution of my writing career.

I was a stay-at-home mom and part-time piano teacher when Bill Buckner, the Director of the Mississippi Fellowship of Christian Athletes and friend from church, telephoned me out of the blue one afternoon. He needed an administrative assistant in his office, and he wanted to know if I might consider it. Duties included correspondence, bookkeeping, and event planning. He complimented my people skills that he had observed at church. I had never worked in an office; I had no computer skills; I really could not even identify most of the standard office equipment. Although I was flattered that he thought of me, I felt totally unqualified and tried to convince him I was not his girl.

He would not be deterred. Promising to get me a tutor, he convinced me to try the job for 90 days. I did, and I stayed three years. During that time, Bill trusted me with composing and writing newsletters and fundraising letters. Not only did I learn the skills I did not have in the beginning, I met a number of influential businessmen who were board members of FCA. Those men played a big role in supporting me when I jumped into publishing a magazine.

From the FCA office, I went to work behind the front desk in two dental practices. Again, I walked in the front door with no background in any of the prerequisites. Along with a lot of jargon about dental work, I learned to file insurance and collect accounts. I met a large community of professionals who were patients. Again, many of them were the very people who opened doors and bought advertising when I started a magazine.

All of those odd jobs appeared to be quite random at the

time. There were days when I thought, "What in the world am I doing here?" A part of me knew that none of those jobs were forever jobs, but another part of me knew that I was where God for some reason wanted me to be during that particular season. It was never about the job—it was always about the people. In hindsight, it all made sense!

I always tell others that everything I know about journalism I learned in kindergarten. When I was a little girl growing up in the Mississippi Delta, my mother was a string reporter for several newspapers. For lack of a babysitter, she frequently took me along as she covered the little towns that ran through cotton country along the rural flatlands of our state.

Her forte was the human interest story. I sat quiet as a mouse while she interviewed any number of individuals who had unique stories to tell. I watched my mother and listened to the stories a second time as she shared them with my father. I learned to love words by hearing her read those stories aloud, and I subconsciously learned that every person has an interesting story to tell. You just have to pay attention!

Forty plus years passed before I had the desire to follow in her footsteps. A lot happened in those decades—not all of it so happy—but I do see that not one thing was wasted. There is always something meaningful to learn if you take to heart the words of Psalm 139.

By midlife, I had hit a few bumps in the road, faced a number of gut-wrenching disappointments and had made the startling discovery that falling on your face is not the end of the world unless you refuse to get up and begin again.

"The Lord will fulfill his purpose for me; your love, O Lord, endures forever—do not abandon the work of your hands" (Psalm 138:9). Never forget that verse.

Gail Pittman, a childhood friend who became a very successful Mississippi businesswoman, began making colorful pottery at her kitchen table for sheer enjoyment. She did not discover her artistic gift until her late 30s. By her mid 40s she had turned that talent into a million dollar business selling her wares in high end stores and catalogs across the country.

Her goal in the beginning was not about starting a business or making a fortune. She just knew that when she molded the clay, shaped it, fired it and painted it, her heart was completely engaged in the process. It is like that when you find yourself using the gifts God gave you. Could that be what it means to glorify God and to enjoy Him forever?

There is a classic movie called *Chariots of Fire*, and it won many academy awards including "Best Picture" in 1981. It tells the story of an Olympic runner, Eric Liddell, who competed in the 1924 Olympics. He was a believer, and his love for God framed every decision in every area of every day. His God given gift was his speed in running. The most memorable line in the movie was this one when Eric responds to an angry sister reprimanding her brother for his attention to running. He replies, "I believe God made me for a purpose, but he also made me fast. And when I run I feel His pleasure." That is what you call a win/win—finding that niche where God desires you to use the gift He gave to you for the purpose of praising Him.

God does give individual gifts to his children. If you pay attention to the song in your heart and the places where you feel His pleasure in the effort, you will discover a deep delight in your own special purpose. God is quite original, and there is no one size fits all. You are the only you.

Corrie Ten Boom was a Christian whose family helped many Jews in Amsterdam escape the Nazi Holocaust during World War II. Her family was eventually discovered and sent to a concentration camp. She survived and started a worldwide ministry for concentration camp survivors. Her book, *The Hiding Place*, tells the incredible true story of her experiences during World War II.

One of the stories she told often as she traveled about and spoke all over the world is the story about a tapestry. She would hold up a canvas revealing the underside, a mass of tangled knots and uneven threads. It was not a pretty sight, and she would ask her audience if there seemed to be any order or meaning in any of it. Then she would show the other side and all the knots and tangles seemed to disappear as a beautiful picture was revealed. Every thread was part of a beautiful picture—a picture which, in this case, was a crown.

Life can look like a disorganized mess at times. There are potholes, detours, and huge question marks. But pay attention. God is always at work. If you are His, you can be sure all those tangled threads, knots, and random circles are working for your good and God's glory. Of that, I am certain.

Be still, and know that I am God.

— Psalm 46:10

You must create more margin so you have room for what's important, not merely urgent.

— Michael Hyatt

Chapter 2

Be Mindful of Your Margins

Richard Swenson wrote a *New York Times* Best Seller in 2004 titled *Margin: Restoring Emotional, Physical, Financial, and Time Reserves to Overloaded Lives*. He defined margin as the space that exists between ourselves and our limits. The fact that it was an instant bestseller and has enjoyed several reprints and revisions over the years suggests that many of us are in need of help. We do indeed live on overload.

Understand that the ubiquitous iPhone did not appear until three years after Swenson's book. Apparently, Americans were struggling with the frantic pace of the daily grind even before we became addicted to text message alerts or notification badges and electronic jingles and swishes that call us to attention constantly.

Our electronic toys have only accelerated and exacerbated the perception of stress all day every day. We have become strangers to the sound of silence.

Musicians recognize symbols called "rests." There are several of them, each distinctly indicating the length of the pause, the number of beats where there is no sound. Those rests, though silent, contribute hugely to the meaning of the music. Silence can be powerful!

My mind goes to the last few measures of Handel's "Hallelujah Chorus." We are sitting on the edge of our seats after the crescendos of the "hallelujahs" coming from every section of the choir. All of a sudden and without warning there is a complete interruption of sound. Nothing. Nothing. Total and complete silence for two beats ... followed by a final huge "Hallelujah!"

It is triumphant and dramatic, and it really doesn't matter how many times you get to experience it because it leaves you as in awe the hundredth time as it did the very first time!

Much of the impact of the finale comes from the fact that it was preceded by the silence. Silence is not powerless. Sometimes, the quietness is the very thing that makes the next thing impactful!

Psychologists and physicians warn us that sensory overload is real, and it is affecting both adults and children. We used to call that phenomenon "Burn Out." There is a sense of nervous exhaustion and a reduced ability to work productively that comes with it. Shorter attention spans, sleep irregularities, and actual structural changes in the brain are the side effects of what one psychologist calls "Electronic Screen Syndrome."

I notice a certain free floating anxiety that is a hallmark of contemporary life. I see it on the faces of the strangers in front of me at the Kroger or the Walgreens. And I see it in myself, too. Surely, we resemble multi-tasking mechanical robots as we stare into our handheld screens and frenetically tap out our communiques to the invisible person on the other end. There is a human connectedness that is slipping away because of our engagement with our devices. This is not good.

Technology is a big offender when it comes to ramping up the stress and speed of life, but it is not the only culprit.

We are blessed to live in an age that affords many opportunities for travel, study, entertainment, and a plethora of experiences that did not exist a hundred years ago. We have a smorgasbord of choices from the day we take our first breath until the day we take our last. So many choices and so many voices can create a daily schedule of complete chaos if we aren't careful! You don't have to do it all or have it all at the same time and in the same season of life!

Dr. Stephen Covey, legendary speaker and author, had a great story that he shared often in his time management seminars. He told of a professor who stood before his class with a large, wide brimmed, gallon pickle jar. The professor carefully placed several fist sized rocks inside, then turned to ask his class if they thought the jar was full. The students were divided in their answer, some saying "Yes" and some saying "No." He then brought out a smaller jar filled with gravel sized rocks and poured them on top of the large rocks. The pebbles filled the gaps between the large rocks, and the professor asked again, "Is the jar full now?"

The students were again divided in their answers. With that, he pulled out a jar of sand and poured it into the large jar, shaking it a bit as the sand filled the few air pockets that remained. Surely the jar couldn't hold anything else. But the professor took a bottle of water and poured it over the rocks and sand until there was no room for even one more drop. The jar was finally full.

The professor then asked the class, "What was the point of that illustration?"

One student guessed, "No matter how full your schedule is, if you try hard, there is always room for one more thing."

"No," replied the professor. "Not at all. The point is if you don't put the big rocks in first, you'll never get them in at all."

The big rocks, of course, are the things that matter most.

Priorities start with your relationship with God. I am sure you have noticed that He speaks softly. If only He screamed at us, we might do better. But He is not like that. And so, He waits for us to notice just how present and willing He is to meet with us. And it's good when we finally realize how very much we need His wisdom and His presence to light the path in front of us.

Priorities like quiet, alone, thinking time, meditating time, praying time to deepen your relationship with God will never happen in your crowded life unless you construct intentional time margins.

There are also those times God prompts us to do something kind for someone else. If there is no white space in the daily calendar, there will never be time for an impromptu act of mercy.

We tend to think that if we aren't praying out loud or quoting scripture, it doesn't really make a spiritual impact on someone else. Not true. When I was diagnosed with breast cancer in 2006, I was on the receiving end of some of the most loving gestures from creative and generous friends. I was single at the time, and I felt very much alone. One friend went to my doctor's appointments with me; another appeared at my door with several pair of brand-new pajamas.

People with maxed out schedules don't shop for pajamas for their friend with cancer or offer to sit with her for hours in a cancer waiting room. They don't have time. Remember; leave some white space for God to use! He will find you, and He *will* use you.

In designing roads, bridges, and buildings, engineers consider margins of safety as they determine the maximum weight a structure can bear. You can be sure they allow a margin between the structure's ideal weight and the weight that would cause collapse.

When we live right up to the line with our time, our resources, and our energy, we are like the bridge in danger of collapse. We are like the jar filled to capacity with rocks, pebbles, sand, and water. Crammed and jammed is not a fulfilling way to approach life.

There is no space left to allow a spur-of-the-moment kindness for a friend in need, no reserve of resources to offer to a cause that touches your heart or to help where there is a desperate need, no reserve of anything inside of us to be the light of Christ in someone else's broken place. In recent years, the expansion of the American Dream has claimed a bit more of the space in the once-ample margin of our lives. Two-career families are the norm. Every family member now needs his own vehicle. There is nothing unusual anymore about families owning multiple homes—a beach house, a mountain house, a weekend getaway condo. Note the size of the average closet in a new home today and then step inside a home built 20 years ago. Closets have evolved. They are the size of a small bedroom, and they are usually quite full!

Consider the self-storage industry. It did not even exist until the 1990s. It is now a flourishing industry with one in every ten American families paying monthly rent for at least one unit. We own a lot of stuff that we have to dust, clean, maintain, or store! At any rate, it can feel a lot like our stuff owns us at times.

In the middle of all that appears to be a sign of affluence and success, there is a troubling reality. Statistics cite anxiety and depression as the leading mental impairments among Americans in 2018. Suffice it to say, something is not working well in the way we do life today.

I believe wholeheartedly that the Creator God lovingly made human beings in His own image. That image means we are so much more than flesh and bone and appetite. We have an eternal soul and spirit that finds its purpose and meaning in our relationship with our Heavenly Father. Trying to live well while ignoring our soul and spirit is very much like trying to build a skyscraper without a ground floor or a foundation!

Sociologists tell us we are living in a secular age; some call it the postmodern age. The culture around us plays to just one aspect of our being, the physical. Our soul and our spirits are, for the most part, greatly under-nurtured by the world around us. Perhaps that soul hunger contributes to our harried nervous pursuit of more activity, more stuff, and more status, more, more, more of that which will never satisfy the thirst inside of us.

I recently read that we cannot give away what we don't have. I think it is also safe to say that we cannot draw from a spiritual reserve we have not nurtured. The noise of modern life works in total opposition to building a spiritual reserve.

The Christian life is a relationship that begins the day you ask God's son, Jesus Christ to be your Savior. All relationships take time, and our relationship with our God is no exception. There are no shortcuts to the kind of faith that stands when all other supports are ripped away. In an age that feels fragmented by so many competing voices, it is a really comforting and rock-solid thing to know that the wisest advice we can follow begins by being still and remembering that He is God. Sometimes, it is easier said than done. Creating that particular margin must be intentional. The noise of the world never stops, and it will always distract us from eternal things. But it is in knowing our Father God that the "being still" becomes a close-to-your-heart kind of discipline you will never want to be without.

And the margins appear like a soft, protective cushion that shields you from the sharp edges of circumstances beyond your control.

Consider this thought from Mark Batterson, the lead pastor of National Community Church in Washington, D.C.: "You need margin to think. You need margin to play. You need margin to laugh. You need margin to dream. You need margin to have impromptu conversations. You need margin to seize unanticipated opportunities."

He does not treat us as our sins deserve or repay us according to our iniquities. For as high as the heavens are above the earth, so great is his love for those who fear him; as far as the east is from the west, so far has he removed our transgressions from us.

— Psalm 103:10-12

Success is never final, failure is never fatal. It is courage that counts.

— John Wooden

Chapter 3

Coping with Failure and Disappointment

Coulda, woulda, shoulda...

Believe it or not, you can find all three "unwords" in Merriam-Webster these days. I just made up "unword" because I am certain my high school English teachers are turning over in their graves about these terms actually being included in real dictionaries.

I seriously doubt a human being anywhere doesn't know immediately that—despite the disregard for the King's English—coulda, woulda, shoulda convey pain and regret with a capital R. They speak of lost opportunities, the sure thing that wasn't, and dreams that died. Welcome to the fallen world where all of our life stories have a few chapters of both pain and regret.

Just so you know up front—loving the Lord and following Him is in no way an insurance policy that protects you from some circumstances that scream, "This is not fair!" Scripture tells us in Matthew 5:45 that "The rain falls on the just and the unjust." Even believers who know better want to complain from time to time, "This is not fair!"

Though I am older, I still have moments when I feel exactly that way. *Alexander and the Terrible, Horrible, No Good, Very Bad Day* is a much loved children's classic by Judith Viorst. Six-year-old Alexander wakes up one morning with gum in his hair, and everything goes downhill from there. No matter how many times I have read that book to my children and grandchildren over the years, I never fail to identify with Alexander. As the day goes on, he becomes quite cynical. In his mind, the whole world is against him! Regardless of our age, we all have days like that, and it's not like we automatically get better at dealing with them as we grow older.

First Thessalonians 5:18 has been a lifesaver verse for me on my "Alexander days." "Give thanks in all circumstances, for this is God's will for you in Christ Jesus." Giving thanks is possible—not because the circumstance is happy—but because God the Father is still in control, and I trust Him even when I do not understand the why of a disappointment.

It is possible to thank Him even then.

I have heard well-meaning adults tell their children, "You can do anything you set your mind to." To be brutally honest, no, you really can't. I could study art with the greatest artist in the entire world, and I could devote every waking hour to painting. I might improve my present ability and advance beyond stick figures, but I am certain I would never become a sought-after artist. There is no raw talent there to develop. I might be disappointed, but I would not call that failure.

Failure is a little tougher because it is quite personal. When I speak of failure, I am describing a darker kind of disappointment.

It involves choosing to do something that you know from the get-go is just plain wrong. Inside your heart, that wise voice, the Holy Spirit, informs you even as you go your merry way that you should turn around and go the other way immediately. But your "prone to wander" heart is stubborn. You proceed, and later regret bitterly that you did not heed the warning. Consequences can be costly. Such failure inflicts a sense of shame, something that has been used by Satan throughout the ages to cripple believers and encourage them to just give up on this whole Christian thing.

Remember well. Failure is a paper tiger with a phony message about eternal hopelessness. It need not mark you for life. We worship the God who not only forgives, but He redeems.

First and Second Samuel tell the story of King David's life. He was the one God chose to rule Israel, the one the Bible identifies as "a man after God's own heart." He was the tender-hearted shepherd who penned our most beautiful Psalms, the courageous young man who went toe to toe with the pagan Philistine giant Goliath, killing him with a simple slingshot and a stone. God's favor was on him, and his love for God evident. At the height of David's power, when everything in his world was going his way, he chose to take another man's wife and then tried to cover up his deed by having the other man killed. What a colossal moral failure. I am sure David's crime would have been the lead on cable news for months if it had occurred today! When the prophet Nathan confronted David about his blatant act, it seemed that the ugliness of what he had done registered completely for the first time. What was he thinking? Had he just tuned out that wise voice in his life in the same way we do? His repentance was immediate, and his grief over his failure was great. His was a huge and well-deserved guilty conscience!

But God's forgiveness was immediate—not because David's sin was small, but because David's repentance was authentic, and God's love was infinite.

David went on to accomplish great things as Israel's king. He learned well from his failure. That truth in itself is part of the redemptive nature of our God. He wastes nothing, even our failures.

David wrote Psalm 51 in the aftermath of that event. It is a transparent and profound plea for a restored relationship with his God. What a precious and intimate picture of what it is to be a broken human being who is wholly humbled by the love of the perfect Father. How merciful and gracious of God to include David's entire story for us to read. It would have been a lovely fairytale if He had omitted that unpleasant episode of personal failure. But God is never into fairytales, and He never wants to leave us with the impression that a relationship with Him is dependent on our perfect performance. Through the ages, David's failure continues to reveal the compassion of God our Father.

In Luke 15, the story of the Prodigal Son tells a very contemporary-sounding story of a young man who was tired of living under his father's roof with his rules and his expectations. He persuaded his dad to give him his inheritance right then and there so that he could leave home to live life on his own terms.

To say the least, his plans fell apart, he squandered all of his fortune, and he found himself penniless and living on the street. He finally returned to his father ready to beg for a job with his father's servants. It was beyond anything he could imagine to ever be accepted as a son after what he had done.

But the son had greatly underestimated the father's love for him. His father welcomed him home with immense joy and celebration saying, "My son who was lost is found!"

I cling to Psalm 139, and I do believe with my whole heart that the omnipotent immutable God of creation does indeed ordain all of our days before a one of them comes to be. Nothing—not even our failures—catch our God by surprise. In verse 16 of Psalm 139 I find great comfort because I know it is true. God knew before the foundation of the world exactly how fickle and frail we would be. He *chose* to love us anyway.

And I also know that Jeremiah 29:11 is true. His plans for us are all for *good* and not for evil and to give us a *future* and a *hope*.

"Come Ye Disconsolate" is one of my favorite ancient hymns. That archaic word "disconsolate" means "without comfort." What an invitation this song is to us in the present moment. Its message resonates. The old lyrics were used in a big contemporary hit, "Come as You Are" by the Dave Crowder band a few short years ago. The original words are by Sir Thomas Moore.

> Come, ye disconsolate, where'er ye languish;
> Come to the mercy-seat, fervently kneel;
> Here bring your wounded hearts, here tell your anguish,
> Earth has no sorrow that heaven cannot heal.

In our secular world that doesn't often acknowledge the power or the sovereignty of God, tuck these timeless words in your heart. They are oh so true.

You see, sometimes in life, the best thing for all that ails you has fur and four legs.

— Mark J. Asher

All things bright and beautiful, all creatures great and small, all things wise and wonderful, the Lord God made them all.

— Cecil Francis Alexander

Chapter 4

Get a Dog to Love

Yes, I really did put this chapter about dogs in this book that is dedicated to my grandchildren. I think God has taught me a great deal about authentic love through a few four-legged creatures, all of whom I hope to see wagging their tails and waiting for me near the pearly gates!

A little personal story here—Charles and I are dog people; we love dogs. When we got married, we each had a Corgi, Daisy, and Thurber. Since I don't believe in coincidences, I am certain that God had a hand in bringing those pups into our lives. Before we even had our first date, our daughters had independently decided we each needed a dog. We later discovered we received them on the very same weekend.

I had recently been diagnosed with breast cancer. My daughter Betsy worried that I was facing chemotherapy alone, and so she gifted me a four-year-old Corgi Rescue named Daisy. Betsy thought Daisy would sit on the couch beside me on my bad days. Charles was a widower, and his daughters just did not like his being alone all the time. Jill and Natalie chose a six-week-old Corgi. Charles named him Thurber after the famous *New Yorker* writer and cartoonist, James Thurber.

We always say we fell in love because our dogs brought us together. A few years later, my son and daughter-in-law were renovating their home in Denver and were forced to move into a rental with three children for an entire year. Their family dog, Dutch, was a Corgi, and they could not find a suitable rental that would also allow them to keep a pet. Charles and I had met Dutch, and we could not bear the thought of their surrendering him to a stranger. It was a joint decision. The Colorado dog became a Mississippian, and we never regretted it.

Those three dogs entertained us every day. They welcomed us home every afternoon with such enthusiasm you would think we had been gone for several weeks rather than several hours. They were on our heels wherever we went, and from our first date through a decade of our marriage, our dogs were a big part of our life together. They lounged around our feet at breakfast, enjoyed pizza and Netflix with us on Friday night, and knew exactly where to look when I said, "Go get your leashes!"

Dutch was the strong-willed alpha dog who established himself as large and in charge. He was more than a little stubborn, and we could never walk away from a plate of "people food" that he did not try to jump up on the table and steal it. Corgis are slightly challenged by their anatomy of very short legs and very long, round torsos. Dutch had an unusual ability to stretch himself like an accordion and reach the bacon on the edge of the kitchen counter! But oh, how I loved that fat Corgi dog with the big doe eyes.

It was a happy and comfortable life we all shared, and I wanted it to last forever.

But one by one we lost our Corgis–Daisy to cancer, then Thurber to cancer, and when only Dutch was left, he stopped eating and became completely lethargic. A few weeks later his blood-work revealed leukemia. We were heartbroken.

We have yet to get another dog. But may I say, I do not regret for one second having loved several dogs in my life. As I wrote in a column once, I would rather live dangerously and cherish the good times than to be cautiously safe and totally miss the joy of love given and received.

I have watched my daughter Betsy love and lose several dogs, too. Her black Lab, Walker the Wonder Dog, was her constant companion through graduate school and her first few jobs. He consoled her through several romances that did not end well, several serious illnesses, several interesting roommates, and several moves. That dog could have been the inspiration for the bumper sticker that says, "Please, God, let me be the person my dog thinks I am."

When Walker was diagnosed with cancer around his tenth birthday, the veterinarian recommended putting him down. Betsy opted for chemotherapy instead, telling her father and me, "You just can't put a price tag on love." And that big hulking dog was grateful. He lived a great quality of life for almost another year. I honestly believe he willed himself to go a bit further because he knew Betsy was not in a good place at the time, and he thought she needed him. I have noticed that dogs are quite perceptive about their master's emotions.

When I visited Paris, my favorite painting in the Louvre was a 22 x 32 foot painting of "The Wedding at Cana" by the 16th Century Italian artist Paola Veronese. There is an amazing amount of detail and symbolism in a painting so large. You can easily find it on the internet, but it will take you several viewings to take it all in. It is just breathtaking. This is the depiction of Jesus's first miracle when He turned the water into wine. I could not help noticing that in the forefront of the celebration are three dogs obviously invited to the feast and lying in repose at their masters' feet. In the notes about the painting is this sentence: "A dog—a symbol of loyalty—lies chewing on a bone." Loyalty. Yes. That is a noble quality, and dogs portray it better than many human beings.

Dr. Derek Thomas, one of my past pastors who is also a renowned theologian, tells me he does not doubt for a second that there will be dogs in heaven. I do believe dogs are part of what God had in mind in Genesis 1:24, 25 when He completed the creation of living creatures and "saw that it was good."

After we lost our last Corgi, the thought hit me as if for the first time that nothing about our life on earth is for keeps. I knew that, of course. The Bible tells us that our lives are "grass," "a shadow," "a vapor," "smoke."

But there was something about saying "goodbye" to Dutch that brought this reality home with such a force the whole concept became personal in a way it had never been before. The years from playful puppy to final breath felt all too few. I wanted more! And isn't that the point? Life is short, and I think the full embracing of that truth is one of the most profound lessons of all.

The reality is that years come and go, and in the gradual day after day, same-old same-old, we don't see the changes dancing in circles around us. But then some loss occurs, and we stop dead in our tracks because that missing piece of everyday has made all of life abruptly different. Losing a four-legged friend is a tender reminder of our own mortality. And even though such a hurt deals a big dose of pain, that brief reflection on the fragility of life deepens our appreciation for the God-given emotion that is love.

James 1:17 says so beautifully that every good and perfect gift is from above. Love is in that category for sure. Family, friends, children, and even dogs—they are good and perfect gifts, yet they are but a preview of the relationships we will enjoy one day when we put on our new bodies in the new heaven and the new earth. The joy and fellowship, at that point, will be without end.

But for this little while on earth … get a dog to remind you.

God is most glorified in me when I am most satisfied in Him.

—John Piper

Comparison is the thief of joy.

—Theodore Roosevelt

Chapter 5

Do Not Compare Yourself with Others

It seems to me there are a lot of unhappy people in the world today. I read a lot of Op-Eds and such in *The Wall Street Journal*, a variety of online news blogs plus the editorial page in our local newspaper. I see many disgruntled men and women of all ages. Somehow, most of them missed the memo that said, "Life is not fair. Play the hand you are dealt and don't waste your energy letting someone else's hand distract you."

I want to scream, "Stop comparing the apples in your basket with the oranges in someone else's. Take what God has given to you and use it in a way that honors Him. I guarantee there is deep contentment in approaching life that way."

As a preschooler in the early 1950s my cultural exposure, though limited, was broader than many of my peers. You see, my family was among the first to own a television set–not because we were affluent but because my daddy sold appliances along with farm machinery in his concrete block building on Highway 82. Only in the Mississippi Delta of that era could you have found such a combination! Our family's single black-and-white TV beamed two Mississippi stations into our living room from 7 a.m. till about 10 p.m. seven days a week. Almost a decade passed before we got a third network! We also had this huge steel antenna that protruded above our roofline, and every time we changed a channel we had to pause for minutes on end while the antenna turned itself to find the new signal.

Ratings were yet to be invented, but everything in those days would have earned a "G" for general audiences. The most popular sitcoms were *Father Knows Best* and *Leave it to Beaver*. The subject matter revolved around traditional families, children who got into a few innocuous kerfuffles, and wise mothers and fathers who managed to turn the small crises into character lessons. To be honest, those programs were not a far stretch from life at our house. There was little room to compare our lives to someone else's glamorous celebrity existence.

What my friends and I knew about the world beyond the city limits of Indianola was almost nil. The *Weekly Reader*, an age-appropriate newspaper we received at school, introduced us to far away countries, and gave us a bare-bones awareness of global issues like hunger and political instability in hard-to-pronounce third world nations. Along with those stories we had some national news of note. "Of note" were things like adding Hawaii as the fiftieth state or the minting of a new penny by the U.S. Treasury.

If there was a pop culture, we did not know about it. Elvis had been drafted—we *did* know that. Those of us with older siblings listened to rock and roll on AM radio. Eventually everyone had a television, and we all tuned in to American Bandstand to see what the kids in Philadelphia, Pennsylvania, were wearing as we studied their dance moves. Otherwise, I doubt we would have learned to "bop" or to "twist" down here in Mississippi.

By the time I was a college student and later as a young married, telecommunications had expanded so much that it did not take any time for a fad, a fashion, or a trend to become a hot item from coast to coast. The world was more connected than before, and it was easier to compare a life in small-town Mississippi with a life in Malibu or New York City. I began to feel a little intimidated in the supermarket checkout line. Glossy magazines bearing the images of perfectly airbrushed models with toned bodies and white teeth and sporting captions that promised "how to" everything in "three easy steps" did catch my eye and make me second guess my life choices. But by that time I was grounded, and despite a momentary "What if," I always landed back at Truth—God's word—and I was okay. I was pretty sure I would not have found life as a Hollywood star very fulfilling.

I am not sure it is as easy to stay grounded today.

Social media has dramatically changed everything about modern life. Much of that change has not been positive. Between Instagram, Snapchat, and Facebook, we see friends and acquaintances posting countless selfies of perfect lives, exotic vacations, and front-row seats to the Super Bowl or the

World Series. The fact that we can Photoshop and edit every detail for the world to see has made it really hard to be content with "regular" when everyone else seems to have "amazing."

I admit that Pinterest is my snare. I have found myself wasting more time than I would like to admit checking out "the right fashion for women over 50," "the best table-scapes for the season," or "the latest in home décor." It's not wrong to care about those things, but it is wrong when the pursuit of such things starts to eat up precious hours, and the pretty pictures start to cloud my reason. My desires collide with my true needs, and I become dissatisfied with everything about my life.

Growing older does not erase the temptation to compare. But age does at least offer a repertoire of memories that help me remember comparison and envy are empty and deceptive.

In the children's classic, *The Velveteen Rabbit*, a very simple little stuffed bunny comes to live in a nursery that is populated by toys that are flashier than he is. In short order, he discovers that he is surrounded by mechanized toys that flash and march and seem to be almost real. Even an adult reading the book to a child finds great empathy for the cloth rabbit who feels inferior and quite ordinary.

From the kindergarten playground to the corporate boardroom, our human ego is prone to measure our worth by some artificial gauge that awards a high score to some and a low score to others. The sting is real when we measure ourselves by that imaginary gauge and realize there are others whose talents, abilities, or possessions are greater than ours.

Comparison has a way of leading to envy, discontent, and the inability to see God's blessings in our own lives. Wallowing in our own self-pity steals our peace and our joy and sidetracks us. We fail to remember God has a purpose and a plan designed uniquely for us.

One of my favorite things about the Bible is how God reveals the unchanging flaws of human character. He did not hide even the more embarrassing episodes of the ancient patriarchs. Comparison is on frequent display. Read the true stories of King Saul's resentment of the young David (I Samuel 16-31). Read about the rancor in Jacob's family with sons who felt slighted by their father's favoritism toward their brother, Joseph (Genesis 37). About a thousand years later, Jesus rebuked his own disciples in Matthew 18 when they began to argue among themselves over who was greatest in the Kingdom of Heaven.

Who is surprised we are still struggling with similar issues today? We have only added to the problem—income inequality, class warfare—even gender warfare. There is just a whole lot of one group not liking another group.

My friend Susan Richardson is a freelance writer and critique reader who wrote almost all of the book reviews for the magazine I published for 17 years. She told a powerful personal story about comparison. Her rescue puppy Libby was still in the chewing stage when she developed a fascination with a particular small potted petunia on Susan's patio. That petunia was one of three little babies Susan had planted side by side in a bucket. Libby did not disturb the other two, only this one. She delighted in pulling it out of the soil and gnawing on its tender leaves. Susan would discover the scrawny limp petunia lying on the concrete and dutifully replant it. This scenario repeated several times over a few weeks. The other petunias were budding and growing larger while this one little plant was having trouble staying alive.

One afternoon as Susan was pushing a lawnmower through the backyard, she came upon that scraggly petunia once again stretched bare on the grass and shriveling in the afternoon sun. Her first thought was to just give it up and mow right over it. She had definitely gone the second mile for this petunia. But something stopped her. She picked up the damaged plant and transplanted it to its own bucket. On a higher shelf, Libby could not reach it. Neither was it dwarfed by the healthy plants. The little plant grew, and one day Susan went outside to discover that the chewed petunia had bloomed.

The sight caught her by surprise, and her eyes welled with tears. She said, "While I stood looking at a single bloom on an undersized plant, filled with pride and joy, the Lord spoke to my heart. He told me that He felt the same way about me as I did about my petunia. He was proud of my blooms and rejoiced over my growth even it might not look that impressive to anyone else."

Susan's past had inflicted its pain. Sexual abuse and persistent bullying in middle school had left her feeling something like that chewed petunia—exposed and stunted. A few years with an excellent Christian counselor had set her on a path to healing. But it was always tempting to compare herself to peers who, like the unchewed petunias, seemed to be thriving in the same garden where she still struggled a bit. "God didn't rebuke me for being uprooted and compare me to a mature plant with no trauma," she said. "He only expected me to grow where I was, not to compare myself with others." She knew God was using that little petunia to tell her something that mattered. It mattered to her heart, and it seemed to matter to God, too. How could she not feel grateful?

One of the best antidotes to comparison is cultivating a grateful heart. I have noticed, too, that thankfulness seems to beget thankfulness. It is as though God gives us eyes to see those significant personal messages—"God-winks" some call them. Start every day reminding yourself of this: "This is the day the Lord has made. I will rejoice and be glad in it" (Psalm 118:24).

The God who tells us in Luke 12:7 that even the very hairs of our head are numbered is the God who also tells us in countless ways how far He has been willing to go to redeem us and to bring us home to Himself. What's to compare?

We are already loved beyond our wildest fantasy.

He who walks with the wise grows wise, but the companion of fools suffers harm.

— Proverbs 13:20

A little consideration, a little thought for others, makes all the difference.

— Winnie the Pooh

Chapter 6

Life-giver or Life-sapper?

I have learned that our daily lives involve a complicated network of friends, family, and acquaintances. Years ago, I remember sitting on a counselor's couch crying over a particular relationship that kept me tied in knots so much of the time. It was not the first time I had sought the help of a professional hoping this time I would learn some secret that had thus far eluded me. I detest conflict, and more than almost anything in the entire world, I wanted to find the magic formula to get along with this person.

On that particular day I learned two hyphenated terms that completely changed my life. It doesn't say a lot about how smart I am to think I had never figured it out on my own. The principles were termed life-giving and life-sapping. Suddenly the struggles I experienced with that particular person made sense. I could even understand the imaginary elephant who parked himself in the middle of my chest every time this person expressed displeasure! I also understood why I was forever walking on eggshells and waiting for the other shoe to drop. Life-sappers tend to have that effect on us.

Life-giving relationships energize, inspire, and refresh. Those relationships are oh so comfortable. Life-giving friends are those we call when we need a soft place to land in the middle of something hard. They are also the friends who celebrate with us when something good comes our way. Jealousy is just not a factor in our relationship, but at the same time, we can count on them to "speak the truth in love," even when it is uncomfortable to hear (Ephesians 4:15).

In total contrast are the life-sappers who strain and drain and never cease to criticize, even in the times when we most need an encouraging word. The world is populated by humans who can be broadly defined as one or the other. This is an observation I have found to be quite true and quite under reported.

As I prepared to write this chapter, I ran across a blog by a Christian author I do love. She had written on the subject of difficult people. I thought it would be helpful to read her take, and it was. Except that she approached the subject from one angle only. She said that if you are having trouble in a relationship, it is because *you are failing* to see the plank in your eye while zeroing in on the speck in your brother's eye (Matthew 7:3).

I agree that a self-inventory is an important first step in figuring out why a particular person causes you so much distress. We can all make it a priority to be more loving and more forgiving and more attuned to the hurts of others. The daily prayer of all Christ followers should be, "Make me more like you, Lord Jesus." However, sometimes you can't help noticing that it is less *your* plank and more *their* speck that is creating the tension. There. I said it, and I mean it.

The Book of Proverbs is filled with practical insights on living well on earth. It is packed with wisdom on relationships and keys to living the good life. Look at these gems.

- *Whoever is slow to anger has great understanding, but he who has a hasty temper exalts folly (Proverbs 14:29).*

- *Wrath is cruel, anger is overwhelming, but who can stand before jealousy (Proverbs 29:24)?*

- *A man of wrath stirs up strife, and one given to anger causes much transgression (Proverbs 29:22).*

- *Pleasant words are a honeycomb, sweet to the soul and healing to the bones. (Proverbs 16:24).*

- *A hot-tempered man stirs up dissension, but a patient man calms a quarrel (Proverbs 15:18).*

- *A gentle answer turns away wrath, but a harsh word stirs up anger (Proverbs 15:1).*

- *A patient man has great understanding, but a quick-tempered man displays folly (Proverbs 14:29).*

- *A fool finds no pleasure in understanding but delights in airing his own opinions (Proverbs 18:2).*

And so it goes. A man of wrath, a hot-tempered man, a quick-tempered man, a fool—I am thankful for these passages. Sometimes the difficult people in our lives are just chronically difficult, and nothing we can do is going to change that. This concept, that there are some who are more comfortable with conflict than with peace, is just a reality to accept rather than to understand.

I am so comforted in accepting that fact because for years, I tried to figure out what I was doing wrong and was sure there was a miracle around the next corner. My miracle did not come although God used that relationship in a myriad of ways to draw me to himself. Christian author and teacher Beth Moore's statement certainly resonates with me: "Sometimes trusting God amounts to making peace with something that won't fix. Sometimes you let it go. Sometimes you hold it broken."

We can't choose our relatives, but we can certainly pick our friends. Life-giving relationships take time and commitment, but the rewards are worth the effort and last a lifetime. My mother, a 1930 college graduate, and her three college suitemates had a tradition called "Round Robin." One wrote a letter, (yes—a real honest-to-goodness, snail-mail letter on stationery) tucked it in an envelope, mailed it to the next friend who added her personal letter. That friend sent it on to friend number three who added her letter and sent it on to friend number four who sent the complete set back to friend number one. For more than 70 years these "girls" stayed in touch that way, sharing the joys and sorrows that wove the tapestry of their lives. They birthed babies, buried husbands, married off children, encouraged each other through joys and sorrows and found great strength through their unconditional love, support and prayers for each other. They lived in three different states, saw each other rarely, were all believers and prayer warriors. Their friendship never faltered because it was built on the firm foundation of shared faith, mutual respect, and unselfish love.

Seek out the life-givers, and strive—even here in the 21st Century—to be a life-giver as well. I read years ago that in the course of a day, at least seven of every ten people you meet are very likely going through something tough. From the barista at Starbucks to the custodian in the school gym to the college student waiting tables at your local lunch place, remember that all human beings have their struggles. A little kindness, a little eye contact, and a little appreciation can be life-giving to someone who is down. Ralph Waldo Emerson made a timeless observation that is as true today as it was 150 years ago. "The only way to have a friend is to be one."

In the very place where God has put us, whatever its limitations; whatever kind of work it may be, we may indeed serve the Lord Christ.

— Elisabeth Elliot

Trust in the Lord with all your heart, and lean not on your own understanding. In all your ways acknowledge him, and he will make straight your paths.

— Proverbs 3:5,6

Chapter 7

Find Your Calling

I have a great affection for my UPS man. Other than the fact that his name is Danny, and he loves dogs, I don't know much about him. I do believe you can tell a lot about people by the way they do their jobs. And Danny does his with a measure of passion and kindness that is noteworthy.

My husband Charles and I are members of Amazon Prime, and that means we can order almost anything without a shipping charge. We do, and the UPS truck makes several stops each week at our house. For more than a decade we owned Corgi dogs who sat side by side at our front door all day long carefully watching the street. They barked at every car, person, dog, or cat that waltzed by.

It never got old for me when I pulled into the driveway every late afternoon and saw those pointed ears and big brown eyes watching for me. As soon as they recognized my car, they would disappear in a flash and go running to greet me at the back door. Each time Danny left a package at the front door, he carefully placed three milk bones on top. It did not take those smart, fat, little pups long to catch on! I would come through the back door, and Dutch, the alpha dog, would continue to bark and beckon with his head as he led me to the front door to retrieve those treats.

Danny carefully bagged a delivery in plastic if there was rain, and he made sure the dog treats were bagged as well. It had to have taken an extra measure of time and care. I noticed.

UPS delivery man is probably not on the list of ten most sought after American jobs. But for Danny, it is apparently about much more than just delivering packages. For believers, it is always about more than a job description. He clearly has a big kind heart, and he has turned a regular job into something that blesses others. That is not a small thing. I just imagine Thurber, Dutch, and Daisy were not his only dog fans!

When we focus on living with integrity and kindness in the small, ordinary moments of life, it matters. When we are faithful to do our best in all our tasks, even when nobody else seems to be looking, it matters. Habits and character are formed in those seemingly unimportant moments.

Our highest calling is to glorify the God who made us. "Glorify" means to praise and worship. Glorifying God is one of those terms facetiously termed "Christianese," the exclusive language of Christians who have an entire vocabulary the secular world pokes fun at. This truth, however, is critical in answering an important question, "What am I going to do with my life?" Colossians 3: 17 says, "And *whatever* you do, whether in word or deed, do it all in the name of the Lord Jesus, giving thanks to God the Father through him" (emphasis mine). That single verse tells me that our lives are not meant to be divided into two compartments: secular and spiritual. I take the words "whatever you do" to mean exactly that—whatever—i.e. everything.

The same God who numbers the very hairs on our heads also placed unique gifts within each of us. When you discover that numbers are easy for you—or that you are really good at drawing a picture or playing the piano or sewing a straight seam or leading a class project—you are starting to discover your purpose. Some of the happiest moments of a life's journey come when we arrive at that "aha!" moment connecting the dots between what we love to do and God's delight in the way we use the talents He has given to us.

Remember well that God uses veterinarians, school teachers, airline pilots, policemen, musicians, and salesmen as well as clergy every day and in every place. He can also use a check out lane at the Walmart or the customer service desk at Office Depot as a mission field. Glorifying God is not a one-size-fits-all single activity relegated to Sunday mornings and occurring within the bounds of bricks and mortar. Serving God is the calling of every believer. There is a delicious joy in discovering the special niche that God designed for you.

Do you realize that God created "work" for Adam and Eve *before* they ever sinned? In the creation story in Genesis 1, the narrative says that God "blessed" man by giving him work to do. In the Garden of Eden, Adam and Eve had a relationship with God, a relationship with each other, and the task of tending the garden. Their work was meaningful and fulfilling. In John 10:10 Jesus's own words speak of abundant life in the present. How can abundant be anything if not joyful?

During those years I published a Christian magazine, I used to see the principle every month. I found this sense of purpose again and again in the lives of those who sometimes stumbled into a passion and then found a calling.

One of my favorite stories was about a very ADHD little boy named Robert St. John who actually flunked out of college and returned home dejected, sure he was destined for eternal failure. He took a minimum wage job in a local delicatessen and discovered he had a natural talent for the entire restaurant industry. Today, he owns numerous successful restaurants, has co-authored at least three coffee table books with artist Wyatt Waters, and regularly leads tours to experience cuisine and art in Tuscany.

Another favorite was the little girl who was eight years old when she saw a documentary about starving children in third world countries. Grace Bateman Greene could barely wait to take her first mission trip to Peru as a high school student. After college graduation she found a job teaching English in Peru, but it was a craft project she initiated for the women in her church there that led to the founding of Peru Paper Company.

She ended up as CEO of a microbusiness that produced a livable wage for countless Peruvian women whose lives were changed by God's prompting of Grace's compassion.

Robert Khayat is the much revered former chancellor at the University of Mississippi. He led the university through a difficult time. His great challenge involved navigating change on a campus where past—yet controversial—traditions were sacred. How could he precipitate change that might be needed, hold on to what needed to be unchanged, have integrity, *and* please the majority of the alumni? He managed to do exactly that, but his backstory makes the accomplishments all the richer. He had grown up as a dirt poor kid from Moss Point, Mississippi. He became a standout football player during his college years when the Ole Miss football team was in its heyday. Later, he was a kicking specialist for the Washington Redskins, and finally an outstanding UM law school professor.

When the law school was shopping for a new dean, however, his peers voted him "not acceptable." It was a hurtful and humiliating experience. Who would have ever dreamed that Robert Khayat would, a few short years later, be exactly the person chosen to lead the entire university through the first steps of needed change as chancellor? He had a diplomatic finesse, and he knew how to listen respectfully to all sides. He was able to bring peace without making anyone feel like they were on the losing side. The first notable part of that entire event is that Robert Khayat possessed great humility. It doesn't require looking very far to see the difficult places that forged that humility.

Finding your niche—the one God made for you—can be like traveling a winding road. Sometimes it is clear, but so many times it is not so easy. There are detours, potholes, and moments that feel like dead-ends.

When my magazine did a cover story on Mississippi artists years ago, I loved what Ginny Futvoye said about the message she keeps in the back of her mind as she is painting. It would be a good thing for anybody to remember whether they are searching for their niche or they have already discovered it. There are timeless words that simplify everything. When asked about her goals and her purpose, Ginny said, "I am brought to Philippians 4:8, 'Finally brothers, whatever is true, whatever is noble, whatever is right, whatever is pure, whatever is lovely, whatever is admirable—if anything is excellent or praiseworthy—think about such things.' When I am painting, the subject matters that I choose hopefully encourage these thoughts."

And when we seek meaning in our toil, may we seek it with those words in mind.

He who dwells in the shelter of the Most High will abide in the shadow of the Almighty. I will say of the Lord, He is my refuge and my fortress, my God, in whom I trust.

— Psalm 91:1,2

The ultimate measure of a man is not where he stands in moments of comfort and convenience, but where he stands at times of challenge and controversy.

— Martin Luther King Jr.

Chapter 8

Prepare for the Storms of Life

On January 15, 2009, a U.S. Airways jet splash landed in the Hudson River with no loss of life, and Captain "Sully" Sullenberger was an instant American hero. The comments we heard from his wife and friends over the next few weeks revealed a man who had been a hero in their eyes for a long time. No matter how many times he was interviewed or praised by the media, he was ever the gracious, humble, and gallant leader who gave credit to his entire crew saying over and over. "I was just doing what I had been taught to do," he said. Sully had been flying aircraft for more than thirty years. I am sure he had persevered through his share of very boring training drills designed to prepare him for the unexpected life and death crisis. But how many routine flights had he made in his career where no special courage or skill was demanded? He might have retired without ever having had to deal with even one tense moment in the air. Would it have still been worth it to put in all the time and effort to prepare for something he wasn't even sure would ever happen? One thing is certain. It would have been too late to read the chapter on disaster management in the flurry of bird feathers heading straight for Flight 1549. No matter how unexciting, Sully had been faithful to do with excellence whatever was in front of him day by day. And in the moment when it really mattered, it was second nature to him to do exactly the right thing.

On one hand, I have always considered it to be one of God's merciful blessings that we can't see exactly what is around the next corner. Our lives are a mix of highs and lows, joys and sorrows. There are times when our planning and effort reap great success, and there are also times when the same amount of blood, sweat, and tears yield an entirely different result.

A few years ago, the Ad Council and the Federal Emergency Management Agency (FEMA) unveiled a campaign with the motto, "You never know when the day before is the day before." It caught my attention right away. The point, of course, was that we don't get an email or a text that tells us that an unforeseen crisis is going to hit us between the eyes and completely upend our lives before the sun sets tomorrow. No. We get up day after regular day without a reason to think today will be any different from the previous day or the countless days preceding yesterday. Life just seems to unfold in a predictable pattern. It is so easy to be lulled into a place where we think that what we see at the moment is always going to be the same.

Oh, sure. On some level we know that we will grow older; those we love will grow older; the pets we love will die one day, and somewhere in the far, far away, life is going to be different from the way we experience it today. "But, surely," we tell ourselves, "that is a long time in the future." And so, we just get up day after day and go through life without a second thought for the day our safe predictable lives might hit a real bump in the road. That is called "failing to plan," and it is not a good idea.

There is a limit to what we can control in the world around us. But there is a vast space within each of us where we choose our thoughts, our beliefs, our ethics—it is in that space our personal character is built. Character becomes the default setting for us. It shows itself in the midst of overwhelming situations when we can barely think a coherent thought—an accident, a grief, a great disappointment.

The unthinkable happens most often when we least expect it. Chuck Swindoll, theologian and author, said, "Life is ten percent what happens to you, and ninety percent how you react to it." How we face those disruptive challenges is largely determined by what we have built into that inner space well before the crisis hit. If our inner space has not been well tended in advance, the results can be devastating.

Gordon MacDonald is a contemporary author I enjoy. In his book, *The Life God Blesses*, he tells this parable that perfectly illustrates that point of tending our character well in advance.

There was once a foolish man who decided to build a sailboat, but not just any sailboat. He wanted it to be the most beautiful boat in the harbor and the envy of all the other boat owners. The most significant and important element in the construction of a sailboat is the part that properly distributes the weight is beneath the water line. That weight in the keel, though hidden from the eye, is the very thing that permits even a small boat to right itself when the winds and the waves toss it about.

But this eager man did not give much attention to the boring and tedious instructions of the boat's unseen portion. He was more interested in spending his money on the colorful sail, the brass fittings, and the polished wood decking. On the sunny morning of its maiden voyage as he sailed out of the harbor, all heads turned to stare. The boat was stunning to behold. The foolish man was quite sure of himself at that moment.

A short while later, the sky darkened suddenly, and a dangerous squall blew from what seemed like nowhere. The monstrous waves swamped the little boat and dashed it mercilessly against the rocks. The very next morning the remains of that beautiful boat washed up on the shore as a pile of rubble. The foolish man was never found.

Gordon MacDonald told an equally memorable story in his earlier book, *Ordering Your Private World*. One morning residents in an upscale Florida apartment complex awoke to the terrifying sight of a sinkhole swallowing their sidewalks, automobiles, lawn furniture, and huge sections of their parking lot. Imagine their sense of helplessness as they watched their whole world literally cave in!

MacDonald explained that sinkholes are the result of underground streams that disappear during a drought leaving the ground on the surface without its underlying support. In so many ways, our modern lives can drift toward a sinkhole threat. The sights and sounds of today's culture will always compete for our attention, but will offer little in substance that nourishes that inner space.

Madison Avenue and your favorite websites will always entice with shiny temptations and promises they can't deliver. Still, it is hard not to notice. Harder still not to believe the hype. Turn off the noise. Pick up God's word. Take a step back, and remember the sinkhole.

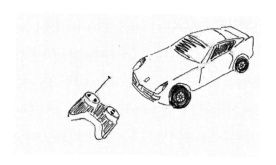

God grant me the serenity to accept the things I cannot change, the courage to change the things I can, and the wisdom to know the difference.

— Reinhold Niebuhr

Never doubt in the dark what God told you in the light.

— V. Raymond Edman

Chapter 9

The Illusion of Control

Life is a never-ending series of seasons, change, and surprises. When Charles and I married in our late 50s, I thought that surely all the things related to a new husband, a blended family, and a new household would be my last major adjustments in life. I also thought it would all be a breeze. I could not possibly have been more wrong.

In the previous four years I had learned what it meant to be on my own for the first time in my life. I had moved out of the home where my children had grown up and had been through a very sad divorce. I had also survived breast cancer at the same time I was starting a new business. It is not my recommendation that anybody follow in my footsteps! But I congratulated myself that those scary disruptive events were all behind me.

Charles and I married on December 29, 2007, at Second

Presbyterian Church in Memphis with all of our children in attendance. On the day after our wedding we headed off to the Grand Hotel in Point Clear, Alabama, for our honeymoon. I remember riding along that endless ribbon of interstate and thinking I was on my way to a new life where there would be no more anxieties, disappointments, and stress—certainly no challenges that could shake this peace and joy that I felt at that moment.

I have always thought that one of God's kindest gifts to us is in not allowing us to see too far into the distance. None of us ever knows exactly what is around the next corner. If we did, we would waste many of the happiest days of our lives focused on that event out there in our future that promises to upend life as we know it. We are meant to hold everything in this world loosely because it is *not* permanent, but few of us live as if we really believe that.

Charles and I had made just a few plans. We would sell both our homes and buy one together. With five adult children between us and the expectation of many grandchildren still to come, we began house hunting for something large enough to accommodate our blended family whenever they wanted to visit. Thinking our homes would both sell quickly, we did not foresee any difficulty in living temporarily back and forth between my house and his.

The famous rock star John Lennon said once, "Life is what happens while you are making other plans." And so it was with us. About the time we began shopping for a home, there was this 'little' very big thing called the Great Recession that wreaked havoc on every aspect of the United States economy. The real estate market tanked. Nobody was shopping for houses. Our "For Sale" signs grew faded on our front lawns as the months passed. The daily drain of trying to keep businesses afloat during a significant financial downturn weighed heavily on both of us. We were enduring sleepless nights and a lot of uncertainty about the future.

I was living out of a suitcase most of the time and trying to find my way around Charles's kitchen every night. There was not one stick of furniture or anything else in his house that was mine at the time, and I felt lost. I look back on my journal from 2008, and I wrote more than once that I felt like I was living someone else's life because I did not recognize mine.

The months dragged on, and this temporary "gypsy" life that we had thought in the beginning would be very brief was becoming our new "normal." There was no end in sight, *and there was not one thing either of us could do to change our circumstances.* I adored my husband, but I was very unhappy with my life. I needed to feel settled, and I wanted my own sense of place. We were very much devoted to each other, but the life we were living was definitely *not* the life we had planned.

The circumstances were slow to change, but I will say that in the interim, we both dug deep into the truths we knew, truths God had taught us in previous trials. After all, at our ages, we had both been through more than a few difficult times. I thank God for the grounding we both had because difficult situations have the potential of causing one's vision to cloud and one's reasoning to go off the rails. We could have easily decided God must not be in this relationship at all and our marriage was a mistake. We never went there.

But we did have to give up the idea of that larger house we both wanted. It was never to be. As grand as it might have been to have lots of room to host Christmases and family-get-togethers, that was just not going to ever happen. Sometimes you just have to let a good dream go.

One of my favorite books that I would want to put on the imaginary "MaeMae's Required Reading List" would be Robert Morgan's *The Red Sea Rules*. Even a person who thinks he doesn't like to read and is not sure God has anything relevant to say would love this book. The ten chapters are short, and the ten points he makes are timeless and very wise life principles.

Rule number one in his chapter called "Cul-de-sacs" is this: "Realize that God means for you to be where you are." Nothing that happens to a child of His catches Him by surprise. It is true that He sometimes allows us to come into difficult places because those difficult places have the potential to do something rich and real inside of us. Nothing painful or challenging comes unless it comes filtered through His loving hands.

In Exodus, when the children of Israel finally marched out of Egypt and away from slavery, they thought their trials were over, and all would be happily-ever-after in short order. Instead, God led them deliberately to the banks of the Red Sea, a place too wide to be crossed and too deep to be forded. Not so far behind them came the army of 800,000 Egyptians in hot pursuit. The Israelites were in an impossible place with no salvation in sight—except for God.

God summoned the wind—that same wind He is still able to command on any given day—and simply parted the waters so that His children walked across on dry land. Remember this— there is never a situation that is beyond God's ability to redeem. He doesn't always change our situation in the way we pray for it to change, but He hears our prayers, and they matter. He is the wise Father who knows what we don't know, and He sees what we can't see. Over time, as years come and go, we look back on our many different seasons of "Red Sea" moments, and we are able to trace His faithfulness.

A few years ago I discovered something I had somehow missed in previous studies of the Book of Ephesians. The Apostle Paul is in a prison cell as he writes this letter to Christians who are enduring horrible persecution. The third chapter contains one of the most moving and beautiful prayers ever recorded. The reader can't miss the profound love Paul feels for these friends, but not even once does he pray that God would take away their trials and tidy up all the miseries in their lives.

Instead he does pray for their strength, their joy, their deep roots, and that they would "know" the love of Christ which surpasses knowledge. I look at that word, "know," and relate it to knowing Charles or knowing my children. It is a level of knowing that is experiential and deep. It is more than knowing a fact like that Columbus discovered America in 1492 or knowing a casual acquaintance by name. "Know" is a beautiful word about a relationship. Paul wants believers to have that kind of love relationship with Christ because that is the kind of relationship Christ wants to have with us.

I think that must have been what Paul had in mind in Ephesians 3:20 when he said that God is able to do in us far beyond all we could ask or dream or imagine. That is what it is to be "filled with the fullness of God." And it's a lot better than that big house I thought I needed!

About a year prior to all of the house drama and decision, I had gone through a season when I felt like God just was not hearing my prayers. Somewhere in a clean up or a purge, I ran across a dog-eared, underlined, written-in book in my mother's library—*Something More* by Catherine Marshall. I love the title. Most of us spend huge amounts of time searching for something more, something we think is better than what we have. How often we find the something more to be something altogether different from that elusive thing we were chasing. The hard things in life—the illnesses, the accidents, the perfect plans that go awry—hard questions, no easy answers are so often the very things that lead us to stare fear or disappointment in the face and find our God to be everything He claims to be.

Catherine writes to all of us, "It is as if God ... says, 'There's only one place and one way you can learn of me, that's just as you are in your present circumstances.'"

Without a doubt, that is a discomfort that is worth every tear.

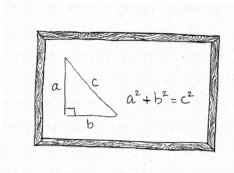

For the word of the Lord is right and true; he is faithful in all he does.

— Psalm 33:4

The truth is incontrovertible. Malice may attack it, ignorance may deride it, but in the end, there it is.

— Winston Churchill

Chapter 10

The Absolute Truth

My husband Charles is now retired, but for 45 years he was in the retail business selling oriental rugs and Country French antiques. He did not start out in rugs or antiques. He joined his parents' floor covering and wallpaper business in the 1970s and was wise to see where the decorating trends were going. There were no other dealers of fine rugs in Mississippi at that time, so he sought out reputable dealers in other places who could teach him about rugs. There was so much to learn, and he says that in the beginning he thought, "How will I ever be able to tell a handmade rug from a machine-made?" To his untrained eye, the fakes looked pretty good to him.

His knowledge grew over time, and so did his appreciation of all that went into creating a fine rug. He eventually decided to travel to India and Turkey because there were things to learn that another stateside dealer could not teach him. From the quality of the sheep wool to the yarn dyeing to the weaving methods to the knot count to the specific designs that gave them their different names—he studied it all.

The more he studied the real thing, the more he learned to appreciate genuine quality and to recognize the true artistry that went into each rug. It was by studying the real thing that he learned to spot the imitation. Today he would be impossible to fool. All rugs advertised as "oriental" are not equal in value.

One of the United States Secret Service's major duties is the detection of counterfeit money. If a bank employee suspects bogus currency, he immediately calls for the Secret Service. Both the bank teller and the Secret Service agent spend significant time during their training learning to recognize fake bills. And do you know how they develop their quick detection skills—by handling the real thing over and over and over? They know the way the paper feels, the unique markings on a bill created at the United States Bureau of Engraving, and the precise placement of every image on both sides.

Whether we are investing in fine rugs, avoiding a counterfeit scam, or wrestling with a serious personal decision, we need to be well informed if we want to avoid a costly mistake. What is true and what is false?

Several months ago as I was watching a highly contentious U.S. Senate Supreme Court confirmation hearing, I heard one of senators say, "That may be his truth, but it is not hers." I could not believe my ears. I thought truth was like math—absolute. Two plus two is four, and it is never going to be anything else.

As much as I would like for it to be five, it simply is never going to happen. I can live with that.

The "his truth" and "her truth" really startled me. Since that day, I've heard that same idea numerous times as "my truth," "conventional truth," or "your truth." Although the acceptance of relativism is not a new concept in our culture, it seems to have gained a much greater foothold in the past decade or so. That fact alarms me.

The perfect example of relativism was that specific comment that caught me off guard during that Senate hearing. A simple definition of relativism is this: Relativism is the belief that there is no absolute truth, only the "truths" that a particular individual or culture happen to believe.

Is that even plausible? So, I suppose I can be a polar bear whether you believe I am or not. Being a polar bear is my truth. Do you see how silly that sounds?

And yet, that seems to be exactly the reasoning of many people in high places these days. I barely know where to begin, but let's start here. If truth becomes a matter of one's opinion, then chaos becomes the norm.

There was a period in the history of Israel after the death of Joshua when God's chosen people did not live in the light of what they had been taught. The Bible's Book of Judges presents a most unflattering picture of Israel, a dark era characterized by idolatry when the people did not faithfully follow the God who had delivered them from slavery and brought them into a land flowing with milk and honey. The very last verse in the Book of Judges sounds like a tragic epitaph. "In those days Israel had no king: everyone did what was right in his own eyes." In other words, "my truth" and "your truth" was the norm. It did not work well then, and it does not work well now.

Truth is still defined in most dictionaries as "conformity to fact or reality." To use a modern cliché, "It is what it is." Back to my example of the polar bear—the unvarnished reality of fact is this: I am not, nor will I ever be, a polar bear.

God's word has a lot to say about truth. Here are a very few verses (emphasis mine).

- *The sum of your word is **truth**, and every one of your righteous rules endures forever (Psalm 119:160).*

- *I am the way, the **truth**, and the life (John 14:6).*

- *Send out your light and your **truth**; let them lead me; let them bring me to your holy hill and to your dwelling (Psalm 43:3).*

- *Teach me your way, O LORD, that I may walk in your **truth**; unite my heart to fear your name (Psalm 86:11).*

God is the author of truth. He is also the source and ultimate standard of truth. Such statements do not sit well with the intellectual relativism that dominates many of America's 21st Century institutions. From the classroom to the halls of government to the multiple platforms of communications and media, there is a constant discounting, ridicule, and open hostility toward those who hold to the belief that God is indeed the infallible source of truth. Our culture at large has a general dislike for authority and absolutes, especially if the name of God is invoked.

Even so, in the same way that my *real desire* to be a polar bear will never turn me into one ... the strident assault by every loud voice denying that God is the one true source of truth will never alter the fact that He is!

Malachi 3:6 says, "I the LORD do not change. ..." His truth does not have an expiration date, and it doesn't evolve with the culture either. As I said before, it is what it is.

In a noisy world filled with competing world-views and opinions, believers must, as never before, possess the discernment to recognize what is true from what is not. First John 4:1 could not be more apropos than in this present day. "Dear friends, do not believe every spirit, but test the spirits to see whether they are from God, because many false prophets, have gone out into the world." Test the voices against God's truth. If you know God's word, you will gain discernment, a most valuable quality throughout your life.

It soothes my soul to read these words in Philippians 4:8. "Whatever is true, whatever is honorable, whatever is just, whatever is pure, whatever is lovely, whatever is commendable, if there is any excellence, if there is anything worthy of praise, think about these things."

I have found this verse to be a sanity saver in the midst of an anxious situation or an unexpected disappointment. I may not be able to control what is happening around me, but I can control where I let my thoughts wander. I can rein in my emotions and remember what I know. The first place I steer my frantic mind is toward whatever is *true*.

There are many good reasons to memorize scripture, but the best one is that its truth will transform the way you think and the way you approach and accept the things life throws your way. God keeps His promises, and He promises to go with His children, to *never* leave them or forsake them. So, right there you know there will *never* be a time or an event in your life when He is not with you. You will *never* be alone. That is a truth that *never fails* to comfort and encourage me.

The Apostle Paul gives the best advice of all time when it comes to living daily in a secular world that is diametrically opposed to a biblical worldview. I love his metaphor of a soldier preparing for battle as Paul explains each piece of armor necessary to face the battle. Ephesians 6:10-18 paints a memorable word picture of a Roman soldier in his battle ready uniform. Each piece of armor protects the soldier in the event of attack by an enemy. The first item the soldier dons is the belt of truth.

The belt was tied in several places in order to remain secure. So, even if the soldier fell down or had to tread on uneven terrain, the belt remained in place. It served a purpose much like an anchor. Imagine a belt with even a tiny missing segment. The belt would be useless because there would be no way to attach it.

And so it is in our relationship with the truth of God. Our trust and belief in His truth must be like the belt—solid and unbroken. Truth is not something akin to a cafeteria line where we choose which portions we want to put on our plate and which items we simply ignore because we do not desire them. All of life turns on what we decide to do with the word, "Truth." It is not always the most comfortable choice, but it is always the right one.

Give thanks in all circumstance, for this is the will of God in Christ Jesus for you.

— I Thessalonians 5:18

Gratitude can transform common days into thanksgiving, turn routine jobs into joy, and change ordinary opportunities into blessings.

— William Arthur Ward

Chapter 11

Gratitude ... Always

I used to tell my son and daughter, "You can't always control your circumstances, but you can control the way you respond to them." As much as I believe that, my response quotient has been better at some times than at others. The thought of giving thanks in all circumstances is presented in scripture as a command rather than an option. Therefore, I do not see any wiggle room. It may just be the most difficult command there is.

There was a very popular book back in the 1970s called *The Road Less Traveled* by M. Scott Peck. The most quoted sentence in the entire book was the first one, "Life is difficult." That is a timeless and profound statement. The book went on to give great advice about avoiding rigidity and giving grace in your relationships. It fell short in its approach to "spirituality," leaning into a relative approach that basically encouraged the reader to find the faith that works for him. (See chapter on Absolute Truth if this sounds plausible to you.)

From the time we are very small, and if we are fortunate enough to have parents who teach us to say our prayers at night, we thank God for many blessings—our mothers, fathers, family, friends, pets … and on and on. It is not hard to say thank you for what makes us happy. It is indeed a blessing in itself to have parents who take the time to teach us the art of being grateful. But, if we live in reasonable comfort—as most of us do—without having a huge unmet need, we can certainly begin to take our blessings for granted. A trip outside our comfort zone to another zip code or another country can frequently awaken our sense of gratitude with a shock of reality. Suddenly our everyday "normal" looks like mountains of gold beside someone else's "normal." Running water and a refrigerator stocked with an abundance of food escapes our notice until we meet someone without clean drinking water or a regular food supply. We find that our taken for granted necessities are someone else's unimagined luxuries. That reality is sobering for most Americans.

This verse in First Thessalonians becomes very uncomfortable when you stop to think about that word, "all," because "all circumstances" can include deprivation and poverty as well as first world problems like divorce and cancer and addiction and not getting accepted to the college you had so hung your hopes on. Not getting something we thought we really, really needed is just part of living in a fallen world. But it still hurts, doesn't it?

Personally, it would be okay with me to never have to deal

with the death of a loved one, even a pet. It would be okay with me to never have to deal with cancer, weeds in the flower bed, traffic jams, taxes, natural disasters, or angry people who shout at other people on Twitter. First Thessalonians 5:18 not only forces us to consider dealing with situations we would rather avoid, it tells us to give thanks in those very places.

I think back to the first part of this chapter when I mentioned *The Road Less Traveled*. That simple truth that "Life is difficult," is like the proverbial fly in the ointment. If we were guaranteed a bit more "yeses" to our prayer requests, it would be so much easier to give thanks in all circumstances, wouldn't it? It is precisely because of the many "no's" we get that makes trying to be thankful in all circumstances so hard.

But God's word says to give thanks in all … all circumstances. Who believes that? No wonder contemporary culture thinks Believers are a bit daft—almost anyone can tell you the world just does not operate that way, thanking God in the middle of discomfort. Of course it doesn't, and that is often the very point God means to make. God intends for His people to be different. He wants that so much that He doesn't leave it up to us to try to manufacture the appearance of being different in our own strength. We have already said that giving thanks in all things does not come naturally. God has not turned the command to give thanks into an etiquette rule, something we just force ourselves to grin and do as well-mannered children. As usual, God is interested in our hearts, the core of our being. He not only wants us to do it, but He wants us to mean it at the same time. He likes real and authentic.

God is the absolute opposite of the good Southern mama who insists that we have the best manners at all costs. He is so not into faking it.

Proverbs 4:23 tells us to "guard" our heart because "it is the wellspring of life." Our actions flow from the thoughts in our hearts. Everything starts there. The greatest distinctive in Christianity is that it is the only religion that operates from the inside out, not the outside in. Something is supposed to happen in our hearts. And when it does, that counter-cultural grateful spirit is released, and it is quite contagious.

Alistair Begg, a native Scot and present pastor of a church in Cleveland, Ohio, gave this this wonderful illustration in a recent blog. If you bump into a person at a crowded party and he accidentally spills his full drink on you, you are then walking around with whatever was in his cup all over your shirt or dress or jeans. If you happen to have a conversation with a thankful person, you are likely to walk away with a bit of his very positive "overflowing cup" spilled all over you as well. By the same token, if you bump into an angry person who curses at you for causing him to spill his cup, you are likely to feel a certain irritation. Those things that bump up against us tend to infiltrate our feelings and behavior. Couldn't we as believers intentionally spill our gratitude cups in a few needy places?

When Jesus uses the metaphors "salt" and "light" to illustrate a believer's influence in the world around him, He is teaching a beautiful lesson. Both salt and light have properties that impact their environment in encouraging ways. When salt is doing what it is supposed to do most effectively, the flavor of the food is enhanced, but the salt is barely noticeable. The salt just has a way of making the food taste better without drawing attention to itself. The same is true of light. When it is most effective in dispelling the darkness, it allows us to find our way without blinding us with its presence.

If we surrender our hearts to God by inviting Jesus Christ to be our Lord and Savior, the Holy Spirit begins a lifelong process in our hearts. It is as though the Holy Spirit gives us a new set of eyes. We learn to see in ways we did not see before, and it's not our determined will power that turns us into kind, loving, grateful people who treat our families and friends and even strangers better than before. Seeing in that new way, however, causes us to do things we may not have done before. Our behavior is different because our heart is different. One of the most notable parts of the transformation of our hearts is a grateful spirit in the face of whatever life throws our way.

This is absolutely not saying that we thank God for a terrible disease or the loss of someone we love. But it is possible to thank God in the midst of the circumstance. He is still sovereign, and He is still in the business of working good in all things that impact one of His own.

I read a touching story of a man who came to that sad place of saying goodbye to a treasured pet. I have been there and done that. Oh, how real is the grief. I identified with the man who said in the middle of his tears, "Thank you, God, for the years you gave me with this good dog. Oh, how we loved each other. Thank you for that. And now, oh Lord, help me to grieve well and then to move forward … maybe to love another."

Only a heart that knows God can do that. Not in its own strength and not leaning on its own understanding (Proverbs 3:5, 6). A heart that knows God, you see, is never in a hopeless situation, no matter what.

When our lives seem to go off the rails and we face disappointment or sorrow and the tears fall and the world sees, we don't have a God who says, "Put on a happy face." Aren't you glad?

But there is a strange gratitude that wells up inside a child of God, one who has steeped himself or herself in His word, and it is indeed possible to have gratitude.

We remember:

- *God's word is true (John 17:17).*

- *He is always working His purpose for our good no matter the situation (Romans 8:28).*

- *He goes with us through every hard place (Psalm 23: 4).*

- *He will equip us to do the things that please Him (Hebrews 13:21).*

It is the truth of God's word that gives us stability in every circumstance of our lives. It is the very knowledge of that same truth that gives us hope, security, and even joy even in the hard places. To know that there is nothing in this world or in the world to come that can ever separate us from the love and care of our heavenly Father—all of the above are the reasons we can give thanks in all our circumstances. It is a sure and supernatural thing.

Faith has a cumulative quality to it. We amass and garner it. We grow it and lay it in store for future times. Our faith grows stronger through the seasons of life.

— Robert Morgan

Be strong and courageous. Do not be afraid; do not be discouraged, for the Lord will be with you wherever you go.

— Joshua 1:9

Chapter 12

Final Word from MaeMae

You know how grandmothers can be. I can't resist the chance to say, "One more thing ... Well, actually, five more things!" And then I am done.

1. Pray ... without ceasing. First Thessalonians 5:17.

Barry C. Black, the 62nd Chaplain of the United State Senate quotes this verse from First Thessalonians and says, "As I grew and matured spiritually, I began to believe that it is indeed possible to pray nonstop. It's possible because we can cultivate a spirit that is habitually devotional, keeping our hearts attuned to the transcendent."

There is a posture, an intentional remembrance that He is God and you are not, that will keep your spirit aligned and your heart receptive. Pray about everything. Your Father in Heaven knows the number of hairs on your head. Don't think for one minute He does not care about whatever is on your heart!

2. Memorize scripture ... it is time well spent.

I confess that I have belonged to several church denominations in my lifetime. I was a United Methodist twice, an Anglican once, and a Presbyterian twice. Charles and I are members of Highlands Presbyterian Church in Ridgeland and presume that this is our final church home this side of Heaven. When I was an Anglican, I loved this one particular phrase that was read every Sabbath Day after the scripture readings: "May God write His eternal truth on all our hearts."

God's words *are* eternal. They are wisdom. They are truth. They do not ever go out of style or become passé like trends and fashion and other elements of culture. There is something about memorizing them. They etch themselves on the very walls of your soul, and when a big unexpected and unpleasant surprise comes out the blue to upend your life, those words pop into your conscious thoughts and they are comforting, healing, and stabilizing. They make sense when nothing else does, and in those times, you do find God to be everything He says He is. So, memorize. Start with the 23rd Psalm, and go from there. You will never ever be sorry.

3. Write thank-you notes ... real snail mail thank-you notes.

Chapter 12 in this MaeMae book was about gratitude. Be sure you read that chapter twice! Thankfulness is a mindset. If you pay attention, and if you follow the first two items on this post script, this thank-you note habit will become second nature. Southerners are big on writing thank-you notes, and that is good as a discipline. But don't just write a thank-you note because your momma taught you to. Be gracious and be thankful and recognize that there was effort involved by someone else who took the time to buy a gift, to send a note, to think of you! Expressing gratitude to those who do thoughtful things for you takes your mind off yourself, reminds you of the joy that thoughtfulness gives to others, inspires you to be thoughtful toward others, and has a strange way of bringing joy to you because you brought joy to someone else. Only God Himself could design a world that works that way. Remember that.

4. Read ... a lot.

As I write this post script, we have just had a major scandal in the country about parents who paid ridiculous sums of money to get their kids accepted to prestigious elite universities. I may be a nobody, but I got an exemplary education from a very small public school system in a very small Mississippi town back in the 1950s and 1960s. I would match my English teachers against any elite school in the country. We were put through the most rigorous grammar curriculum year after year after year. Not a one of us struggled to know whether to use "I" or "me" correctly in a sentence … ever. Learn proper English rules.

You don't have to go to an elite school to prove you are smart. Is that clear? An impressive school name on a diploma will never compensate for poor manners or ignorance in history or cultural literacy.

Read widely and read well. Read biographies of noble historical figures—all of them. Read about Washington, Jefferson, Lincoln, Churchill, and others. Learn history. Learn especially about World War I and World War II and the sacrifice of American lives for the cause of freedom. We are living in an era where many want to take down monuments, to erase parts of history that aren't pretty. The Civil War was not pretty, and slavery was not pretty, but removing the monuments is not pretty either.

God did not leave out the unflattering parts of biblical history. In reading the stories of the patriarchs, we see every failing imaginable. It is quite an R-rated scenario. Why did God not leave out the parts of the history of Israel that reflected poorly on their loyalty to their God? We can be encouraged by the fact that He did not gloss over those parts.

We learn to not repeat history by knowing history. Pretending the un-pretty parts never happened does nothing to insure a prosperous and different future.

Love reading because reading opens doors and opens your mind. Read. It is never time wasted.

5. Don't believe everything you hear on the news.

We live in an era when the words, "fake news," are flung about among politicians and news pundits every day. If you listen to one group, you are sure to think the world will end before the sun sets tomorrow. Another group will tell you the world has never been in better shape. Be informed, but be wary of accepting at face value everything that comes across the air waves.

And if the news begins to cause you fear or alarm, see number 2, and never forget, "The Lord is *your* Shepherd." You will be fine.